Personal Par
A Psychological System
Of Golf For Women

Barbara K. Keogh, PhD
University of California, Los Angeles

Carol E. Smith, PhD
System Development Corporation

Human Kinetics Publishers, Inc.
Champaign, Illinois

Production Director: Karen Morse
Typesetters: Carol McCarty and Sandra Meier
Text Layout: Janet Davenport
Cover Design and Layout: Laurie J. Paul, Images
Illustrator: Steve McAdam

Library of Congress Cataloging in Publication Data

Keogh, Barbara K.
  Personal par.

  1. Golf for women—Psychological aspects.
I. Smith, Carol E., 1918-   . II. Title.
GV979.P75K47 1984   796.352'024042   84-22444

ISBN: 0-931250-92-7

Printed in the United States of America

10 9 8 7 6 5 4 3 2 1

Human Kinetics Publishers, Inc.
Box 5076
Champaign, IL 61820

Contents

Preface

Personal Par: A Psychological System of Golf for Women was written for women who like to play golf and who want to play better whether their average rounds total 85 or 125. If you are really addicted to golf—and many of us are— you read words, follow diagrams, and watch television for clues of how to shave off strokes. The problem is, most advice on golf is directed at men and focuses on golf techniques. *Personal Par* is written to women and is concerned with the psychological side of golf.

The book grew out of an invited lecture that author Barbara Keogh gave to a group of LPGA teaching pros at Pebble Beach in 1980. As with most books and most golf games, the content has gone through a number of trials and revisions. The two authors have been the primary subjects in these experiments, and we are pleased to report that the Personal Par system works. Since using the system we have played better and enjoyed the game more. We wish to thank Jack F. Keogh for his continuing interest, patience, and help as *Personal Par* grew from an idea to a reality.

Personal Par is based on the principles of psychology. Playing within this system will lead to better performance and to more enjoyment of the game. The system allows you to use your skills by controlling and directing your golfing motivations and tensions; it will help you set positive and enhancing playing goals; it will improve your concentration and attention; and it will help you understand your own expectations and aspirations. *Personal Par* puts you in charge of your game.

Teeing Off

This book is about a system of Personal Par and how to use it to your advantage. The system is based on psychological principles which have been shown to work in laboratories, clinics, classrooms, and on the golf course.

A central theme throughout is that most women will enjoy golf more and will score better if they change their psychological approach to golf and are psychologically in control of their games.

Psychological control involves a number of things: understanding your reasons for playing, understanding the psychological tensions which enhance or disrupt performance, and understanding your own reactions to these tensions. It means understanding how to control pressure and how to use tension to improve your performance. Psychological management is a key to enjoyment of the game and to good play. If you want more satisfaction from golf, concentrate on the aspects of the game that you can control—your own perceptions of the game and your own psychological approach to it.

A Many Splendored Game

Golf is a game to be enjoyed. It is a chance to disengage from the everyday demands of family and job. It is a chance to feel the damp, rich springiness of putting greens, to take in the subtle smells of grass and rough, to observe the effects of seasonal changes on familiar terrain.

Golf is a sensual game, a game of feeling as well as of technique. Golf increases our sensitivity to sounds, to sights, and to the feelings of our own movements.

Golf is also an intellectual game. Outside problems must be shut out. The immediate situation demands attention. It is a game that forces us to identify the task at hand and to analyze our own skills for getting that task done. Golf stretches our ability to think.

So What's the Problem?

Why then is golf such a frustrating experience for so many women? It is because we concentrate on the wrong aspects of the game. We get caught up in the technical, physical, and mechanical parts of golf. We ignore the intellectual and psychological components; and, as a result, we wind up with more strokes and less fun.

True, golf *is* a physical game. It does require certain levels of strength and coordination, and it does require specifics of techniques. No doubt most of us could improve the physical and technical aspects of our games if we took more lessons, practiced daily, and played golf four times a week.

In real life, however, golf usually takes a back seat to family needs, to work demands, and to limits on time and money. Most of us think about golf more than we actually play it. How to think about your golf game and how to manage your game psychologically—that's what this book is about.

However, don't be misled. This book is not about stance or grip or swing. It doesn't show you how to fade a shot or put overspin on a ball. Technical aspects of golf are the province of teaching professionals. This book is about the *psychology of golf.*

Our purpose in this book is to help you gain psychological control over your game. So, by way of background, let's identify some of the psychological factors that affect performance.

Why Don't I Play Better Golf?

Sad but true, most of us don't perform as well on the golf course as we could or sometimes feel we should. Even when we take our limited physical skills into consideration, we don't play near our potential. The problem of playing to potential is present in all games and at all levels. You've seen an expert football player drop a sure touchdown pass, a world-class tennis player muff an easy lob, or a touring golf pro miss a two-foot putt.

Whatever their levels of expertise, all performers make mistakes, have good and bad days, and are sometimes affected by pressure and tension. High-level performers have learned to control and direct their psychological energy in order to minimize disruption. Less skilled performers—the vast majority of the world's golfers—are especially vulnerable to psychological disruptions. The trick is to learn to control and to use these psychological influences so that they improve performance rather than disrupt it.

Is It All in My Head?

Golf is not just a psychological game, of course. Kinesiologists and physiologists who study sports and sports performance are interested in the physical, neurological, and biochemical aspects of motor performance. In their laboratories, these researchers test changes in such factors as muscle density and blood chemistry levels. Their findings are especially important for the high-level competitive performer because many physiological and biochemical conditions contribute directly to peak performance on a given day or in a given match.

For most of us who play at much lower levels of skill and competition, the psychological influences on performance are often more important than the physical or physiological ones. We do not play as well as we might because of our psychological approach to the game. Most of us don't have the time, energy, or commitment necessary to change our physical coordination or our strength. However, we can do a great deal to improve our mental set and our psychological control over our games, accomplishing this relatively quickly.

Let Psychology Help!

Personal Par is a psychological system for managing yourself as a golfer. It is a way of thinking about golf and of helping you to analyze your game in order to identify strengths and weaknesses, to set goals which optimize performance, and to select effective playing strategies. Personal Par provides you direction for lessons and practice both on and off the golf course, and it prepares you mentally to play.

From a psychological perspective, the most important thing about the system of Personal Par is that it puts you in control of your game. This does not mean that you will get rid of all of the frustrations and disappointments in playing golf, but rather that you will use psychology to your advantage on the course. The result will be better play and lower scores. Most importantly, it means you will have more fun playing golf. This is what it's all about.

Preview of Coming Attractions

In the first chapters, we briefly discuss three topics in psychology which are especially important for golfers to understand: Motivation, Anxiety, and Attention. Then we describe the numerical basis of Personal Par and show you how to compute your personal pars on a hole-by-hole basis. We also demonstrate how you can use the Personal Par system for wiser strategy decision, for better club and shot selection, and for greater understanding of your own abilities as a golfer.

Finally, we show how playing the Personal Par system will give you insight into what and how to practice, how to choose a pro, and how to think about golf when you are away from the course.

If you're the impatient type, jump right in. Start by computing your Personal Par and playing. Then come back to find out why it works.

If you like to look before you leap, take the chapters in order and then apply the system to your game. We'll begin by talking about the three psychological influences on performance: Motivation, Anxiety, and Attention.

Motivation
And Golf

Most of us think of motivation as meaning wanting to succeed, "trying hard," and expending a great deal of energy. Remember how much energy it took to complete a round when you played poorly? Remember how tired you were after a 4-hour round of catch-up golf? Trying hard is one thing most of us do well. Alas, trying hard is not enough. Powerful aspects of motivation influence your performance on the course. Understanding them will lead to improved play and to more enjoyment. First, consider your motivation for playing golf.

Why Do I Play Golf Anyway?

How many times have you asked that as you struggled in after a sloggy day on the course? Nothing seemed to go right. You played badly, and you had a big score. With the exception of a few good shots, your golf was dismal as were your spirits. All golfers have days like that, and occasionally, all of us think about giving up the game. Yet most of us don't. In fact, most of us eagerly look forward to our next chance to play.

What Keeps Us Coming Back?

Why do we willingly submit to hours of frustration as often as we can? Examining and understanding your motivations for playing will help you take charge of your game psychologically, for being in charge is what's important.

Think about the golfers you know. They play golf for different reasons—all good reasons, but different. Some women play to have time with their husbands. They enjoy golfing vacations and weekend time together on the course.

Other women play golf because it is a social game. They like to be members of a club, to be part of an active social group. Being part of a social group is important for all of us, and for many women golfers, it may be a major motivator for regular play.

Alone at Last!

For some other women, however, golf is a chance to get out of social demands. It is a way to be alone, to think about oneself, not about others. Golf may provide a brief oasis of quiet in a hectic schedule filled with family, friends, and work. For these women, it is not the chance to be with others, but the chance to be away from others that motivates them.

Still other women play golf because it is an opportunity to be involved in a competitive activity. For many women, whatever the size of their handicaps, competition is fun, and they play golf because they like to compete. But competition, even in low-key club tournaments, is not for everyone.

From a psychological perspective, then, it is clear that there are many motivations for playing (sometimes enduring) golf. It is likely that your motivations are overlapping, because at different times in your life, you play for different reasons. It is important for you to understand your motivations, to recognize what it is that attracts you to the game, and to understand what it is about the game that brings you satisfaction.

Analyze your own feelings about when you play, where you play, and with whom you play. These feelings will provide some insights into your motivations for being a golfer.

Unfortunately, most of us are not good analyzers of our own motivations. As a consequence, a golfer who doesn't like competition may find herself playing too many rounds in a highly competitive foursome; or one who enjoys competition may end up regularly in social groups. In either case, the golfer does not find the game satisfying. Importantly, she does not feel in control.

The reasons you play affect how you play as well as how much you enjoy the game. If you like competition, even relaxed competition, play with people who like to compete. If playing competitively bothers you, if you prefer a more social time on the golf course, choose playing partners who also prefer the social to the competitive side of the game.

Why Oh Why?

Understanding our reasons for playing is only one aspect of motivation which affects our play. We are also influenced by the attitudes we hold about ourselves, especially the attitudes we have about ourselves as golfers. One way to gain insight into these attitudes is to examine the interpretations and attributions we make about our play. Fortunately for golfers, self-attitudes and attributions have been major topics of study by psychologists whose findings are directly relevant to improving our play.

Why Did She Do That?

Attributions are the interpretations or inferences we make about the causes of behavior or events. We try to "make sense'' out of the events in our lives by understanding their causes. We act according to these attributions or explanations. Psychologists who study personality and motivation suggest that our attributions about the causes of behavior determine in part how we feel and how we act.

For example, we forgive a friend's curtness on the phone if we attribute her behavior to a headache; but we're offended and hurt if we attribute the same behavior to deliberate rudeness. We're pleased and satisfied if we beat a skilled bridge player in an important match; but we're disappointed and dissatisfied if we won because our opponent gave us the game. We excuse a child's misbehavior if we attribute it to fatigue; but we are irritated with the same behavior if we view it as pure mischief.

Why Did I Do That?

In addition to making attributions about other people's behavior, we make many interpretations about our own. This is true on the golf course as well as at home. Attribution theorists suggest that our feelings of pleasure, pride, and satisfaction, as well as our behavior, are determined in part by the reasons we give to explain our own or other people's behavior. When people strive to perform well in the classroom or on the golf course, they are apt to attribute success or failure to four major causes: ability, effort, luck, or difficulty of task. Whether we feel happy and proud about our successes or sad and angry about our failures is related to the attributions we make to explain what happened.

Pupils in school feel good about a high grade on a test when they attribute the grade to their own ability and hard work; they feel less pleasure or pride when they view the grade as due to an easy test or to luck. Interestingly, too, a good grade attributed to ability and effort leads to increased effort and greater persistence on the next assignment. When a good grade is attributed to luck, there is little change in subsequent behavior.

Who's in Charge?

Attributions have powerful effects. Our attributions contribute to our enjoyment and affect our self-confidence.
Consider the impact of similar good rounds on two golfers.
One attributes the score to her diligent practice; the other
attributes the good score to a lucky day. Predictably, the
good score for the first golfer will lead to greater confidence, increased effort, and willingness to practice more.
Predictably, the good score of the second golfer will have
little impact on her self-image or on her practice or effort.
In the first case, the golfer felt responsible for her own
good play; in the second case, the golfer felt her good play
was not under her own control.

The idea of feeling responsible or in charge of your game
is an important aspect of motivation. Psychologists refer to
these feelings as *locus of control*. In a broad sense, when we
view the outcome of an event as under our own control, we have an *internal* locus of control. When we view
the outcome of an event as beyond our control, we have
an *external* locus of control.

Comme ci, Comme ca

People are not all internal or all external in their locus of
control, of course. If we think of our daily lives, it is clear
that we have an internal or external locus of control for different things. We may feel "in charge" in some situations
but not in others. One person may feel confident and
capable when starting to prepare a gourmet dish, knowing
that her cooking skills will guarantee a fine result. In the
same situation, another cook may feel apprehensive and
unsure, viewing a successful outcome as chancy. The roles
may be reversed, however, when the two individuals sit
down to help their sixth graders with a difficult arithmetic
assignment or when they are asked to organize an execu-
tive conference.

The point is that we have different perceptions of our
control over events in our lives. Importantly for the golfer,
we also have different perceptions of control for our suc-

cesses and for our failures on the golf course. One person may feel responsible for failures but not for successes, while another person may have the opposite feelings about success and failure.

Some Cases in Point

Can you recall your playing partners' comments after hitting bad shots? One may say, "I don't know why I take lessons—I'll never be able to play well." Following a similar poor shot another may remark, "I usually hit that shot well. Too bad the lie was so bad." When they each hit a good shot, the same two golfers may comment: "What a lucky shot" or "My lessons are really beginning to pay off." These differences in attributions or interpretations of good and poor shots tell us something about the psychological approach each golfer brings to her game.

I Think, Therefore, I Am

If you come to the course feeling in charge of your game, you will interpret a good shot as due to your own skill, effort, and concentration, and not just to luck. You can write off a flubbed shot as due to a bad lie or to a temporary breakdown in concentration or swing. You feel confident, and you are not devastated by a single bad shot, hole, or round. Importantly, too, every good shot or round enhances your confidence and increases your sense of being in charge.

In contrast, if you feel your golf game is mostly a matter of luck (sometimes good, sometimes bad), you gain less satisfaction from good play. Solid shots are viewed as lucky flukes while poor shots may be interpreted as more evidence of your ineptness as a golfer.

It's not just the shots themselves that are important psychologically, but how they are interpreted. Analysis of your own attributions will shed light on your feelings of control about yourself as a golfer.

What Do You Expect?

Many women golfers come to the course expecting to play poorly—and indeed this expectation is often proved true. High scores are due in part to limited physical skills. High scores are also caused by lack of confidence and low expectancies.

Expectancy is an aspect of motivation that affects many areas of our lives. Expectations influence our psychological approach to an activity or task and also influence how effectively or how well we perform. Educational psychologists who study children's learning and achievement have shown that some pupils perform poorly in classrooms not because they are intellectually dull, but because they expect to fail. This is called a *self-fulfilling prophecy* and is as relevant on the golf course as in the classroom.

Excuses, Excuses

Listen carefully to first-tee comments of your golfing partners. "My back is bad, I can't take a full swing" . . . "I haven't played for two weeks (or months? or years?)" . . . "We had weekend guests and I'm exhausted." Gamesmanship? Sometimes, perhaps. But most of the time these comments are rationalizations for expected failure. They are ways we protect our egos from public humiliation. They tell us about the psychological expectancy of the golfer. Many women have a negative image of themselves as golfers. They lack confidence, and they expect to play badly. As a consequence, they often play below their potential.

Dreaming the Impossible Dream

It is paradoxical that although many women have poor concepts of themselves as golfers, they set unrealistically high goals for their own performance on the course. They come to play with the view that they are poor golfers, yet they set an unachievable goal—par—as their standard for which to strive. As we will show later, acceptance of par as the most important standard of success often leads to feelings of failure and to poorer rather than to improved play.

A Lesson From the Classroom

From extensive psychological research in the classroom, in the laboratory, and on the sports fields, we know that realistic and positive goal setting leads to increased effort, to greater willingness to persist at an activity, and to improved performance. Students have little reason to try hard or to persist at an activity if they are convinced that they are going to fail anyway. Golfers and students are alike in this regard. We can apply the lessons of the classroom to the golf course.

We have already described how attributions have an impact on your performance and on your enjoyment of golf. Expectations and attributions are clearly linked. Setting unrealistically high goals often leads to attributions to luck when we are successful and to self-blame when we fail. On the other hand, setting unrealistically low goals takes away the value of success and makes failure even more devastating psychologically. Think how much more satisfy-

ing it is to play a difficult hole well than it is to score low
on an easy hole. By the same token, it is more frustrating
to blow an easy hole than a difficult one.

Know Thyself

Analyzing your own goals and expectations will provide
you insights into your motivations which will affect your
golf performance. You may find that you set unrealistically
high specific goals yet have a generally low expectation for
your game. When you understand how your specific goals
influence your self-image as a golfer, you can make the
self-fulfilling prophecy a positive rather than a negative
one.

Anxiety And Golf

A second powerful influence on performance is anxiety or tension. Let's recognize immediately that golf is a tension-producing game—fun, but tense. First, golf is public. A bad shot is visible to anyone who happens to be watching. You can't hide it and you can't take it back. All you can do is regret it, feel embarrassed about it, and remember it.

Second, golf is a game which leads to an objective numerical outcome: the score. You know and everyone else who sees the score knows something about how you played that day. Seldom do you do as well as you hoped you would. Even when you play smoothly and easily, you may not score well, so you may come to the end of the game feeling upset and disappointed.

Third, golf is a cumulative game—everything counts. You have to play 18 holes. All it takes is one disastrous hole to ruin your score for the round. A 4 putt here, an OB there, or two balls in the water really hurt.

The publicness, the objectivity, and the cumulative demands of a round of golf all contribute to psychological stress: to tension and anxiety. Because golf is important to us and because we care about how we do, we invest a lot of ego into our games. We are achievement motivated; we want to play well. At the same time, we are unsure about how things are going to turn out; disaster lurks on every hole, on every shot. Psychologists have shown that the combination of importance and uncertainty produces anxiety.

Often it is tension and anxiety, rather than your physical skills, which disrupt your performance on the course. For you to improve your game, you must learn to control and to direct your golfing anxieties. You need to understand the nature of the relationship between anxiety and performance, and to understand the sources of anxiety.

Who's Uptight?

All golfers have experienced first-tee jitters, a feeling that comes as you pray that you won't mess up that first drive while casts of thousands (waiting golfers, the starter, your playing partners) watch in silence.

Unfortunately, anxiety isn't left on the first tee. It appears all over the course. Ever get butterflies in the stomach as you address an ''easy'' three-footer to finish a good round? Ever feel nervous as you step up to hit a short iron that you've got to have to win a hole in match play? Ever tighten up when faced with a shot over water or sand? Of course you have! We've all added strokes to our scores and bruises to our egos by letting our tensions get out of hand. We have let anxiety disrupt us. One big step toward better golf is to learn how to control and how to use your anxiety.

Psychologists have studied anxiety for many years. Psychotherapists in the clinic and experimentalists in the laboratory have documented the impact of anxiety on human beings. Anxiety is not just a feeling; it is not just in your head. There are many physical and physiological indicators of anxiety: changes in heart rate, in pupillary dilation, in respiration, and in sweatiness of hands. Indeed, it has even been proposed that these physiological changes cause our feelings of anxiety.

Sports psychologists now suggest that anxiety is manifested in two forms: *somatic* and *cognitive*. Although a few specific situations or stimuli may trigger complex physiological reactions which lead to cognitive worry, most anxiety is cognitively based. It is self-doubt and concern about performance that makes us anxious and which leads to the somatic signs of anxiety. Within limits these changes are not bad; in fact, they may enhance our play.

Sweaty Palms?

Physiological psychologists refer to physical changes as arousal. They make the point that the effect of arousal is to get a person ready to perform. We need certain levels of arousal to prepare us to play. One of the important concomitants of change in arousal level is change in attention. We attend better, concentrate better, and use information better when we are at optimal levels of arousal. Anxiety, arousal, and attention are all important contributors to performance on the golf course.

The relationships among anxiety, arousal, and performance are complex and vary according to the skill level of the performer and the performance level demanded. Because of our psychological perspective in this book, we will consider anxiety as the emotional or cognitive expression, and arousal as the physical or somatic expression of the same psychological process. We refer to both terms when we describe how these processes affect performance.

How Many Butterflies Are Enough?

An important psychological finding for a golfer is that performance actually improves when you are moderately anxious or aroused. The fact that you feel tense before taking a shot tells you that you are involved in the game, that you care about how you do. You wouldn't be tense if you didn't care how you hit the ball or where it went.

Little anxiety or low arousal means no involvement. You are bored. If you don't care about what happens, the usual result will be poor performance and high scores. On the other hand, if you are too uptight, you will choke, muff shots, and, alas, you will score high.

The important point to remember is that *some* anxiety leads to improved play. Your goal is not to get rid of anxiety but to control and direct it. One way to think about anxiety control is as energy management. You want to manage your psychological energy so you are in your optimal energy zone. You want to avoid extremes of boredom and uninvolvement. You want to avoid overwhelming and disruptive tension.

When you are in your optimal energy zone, you function best: You are up for the game. Your attention is sharp, you feel in control, and you are ready to play. Some athletes refer to this as being in their "flow," the level where performance seems smooth, effortless, and complete. Being in the flow is primarily psychological not physical, so we need to think about how to control and direct our own psychological energies.

The Upside-Down U

Psychologists tell us that in a general sense the relationship between anxiety and performance can be shown graphically as an upside-down U. The anxiety/performance relationship looks like this:

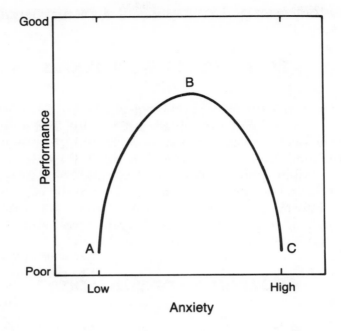

Low to high anxiety is plotted along the base line of this figure. Poor to good performance is plotted along the vertical line. Look at the curve that is formed. It clearly shows that anxiety and performance are related.

Performance is poor when there is too little involvement or arousal (Point A) and deteriorates when there is too much anxiety (Point C). Obviously, best play comes in the middle range (around Point B). Here you are into the game; you are involved. You may feel tense, but you are in control of your tensions rather than having your tensions control you.

For most golfers, generating enough anxiety is not the problem. We are seldom bored on the golf course. Most of us are deeply involved in the game and want to play well. Our problems with anxiety and tension are on the other end of the scale. Because we are overanxious, our anxieties disrupt our play. In order to improve performance on the course, we need to understand what leads to optimum levels of tension and what causes disruption of performance.

What Makes Me Anxious?

Golfers can learn from psychologists who have studied anxiety in the laboratory, in clinical practice, and on the athletic field. The evidence shows that both the importance of the outcome and the uncertainty about the outcome lead to anxiety in sports. Golfers need to think about at least three sources of disruptive anxiety: Unrealistic Goal Setting, Information Overload, and Ambiguity. All of these factors lead to poor performance, high scores, and frustration. Let's take a look at them, one at a time.

Reaching for the Moon?

Psychologists have conducted many studies of the effects of goal setting on individuals' performances on a variety of tasks and in many different situations. The findings are clear: Performance deteriorates when large discrepancies exist between our goals and our abilities. When our goals are too high and, thus, are unreachable, we feel discouraged and frustrated, and our performance deteriorates. Our anxiety increases as our uncertainty about the outcome is greater. When our goals are too low and we do not feel challenged, we soon become bored and our performance goes to pot. Think what this means for golfers.

Are You Really a Par Golfer?

Most of us have set unrealistic goals for our golf game. In your fantasies, do you see yourself playing par golf, having occasional flashes of brilliance that net a subpar round, dotted with birdies or unexpected eagles? Do you follow the play of the touring pros and rejoice or commiserate as their scores vary around par? Most of us aspire to be scratch golfers or par shooters. We have so bought into the power of that magical value—par—that we view any score higher as failure.

The cold reality of golf statistics shows us that fewer than 1% of the estimated 5 million golfers in the United States are regular par shooters. The average score for most golfers is more apt to be in the 90s or 100s than in the 70s or 80s; rounds recorded under 90 are the exception, not the rule. Based on these rather surprising statistics, most of us can expect to play regularly at 20, 30, or 40 strokes over par. That means we'll be recording scores in the 90s and 100s, not in the 70s.

To set your goals at par golf, to define success or failure in terms of par is both unrealistic and self-defeating. Your enjoyment of the game is related to the goals you have for your own performance as well as to the actual level of your golfing skills. Most of us aspire far beyond our physical abilities and technical skills. Our goals are unreachable. As a consequence, we seldom play within our optimal energy zone. We seldom experience a state of flow because of the discrepancies between our abilities or skills and the goals or challenges we set for ourselves. We finish a round feeling unsuccessful and disappointed. Remember the frustration and self-anger you felt at being "2 over" on a par 4 hole? Yet, honest self-evaluation might reveal that you can make a 4 only with the rarest of good luck. Indeed, a 5 might be a reasonable goal for you on that particular hole.

Not So Viva la Difference

The consequence of a large discrepancy between goal and performance is tension, frustration, and anxiety. Golf is like other human activities, and the psychological laws which govern our behavior apply on the golf course as well as at home, at work, in the classroom, or in the psychology laboratory. The best performance is achieved when there is a realistic discrepancy between the goal to be accomplished and the skill level of the performer. We direct our energies best when there is a match between our capabilities and the challenge in the task.

Too Many Bees in Your Bonnet

Unachievable goals aren't the only things which lead to disruptive tension. When you try to deal with too much information, when you are "overloaded," you don't perform well. Your processing system breaks down. It can happen anywhere. You may forget important facts, you may make poor decisions, or you may perform ineffectively and inefficiently.

Information processing—how individuals learn and think —is a major area of current psychological research. From this research, we find that humans have a limited capacity for the amount of information they can process at any one time. From the research of neurologists and neuropsychologists, we know that the human brain processes information in many different ways. For most people, language is processed in the left cerebral hemisphere; tactile information is processed in the right. The left hemisphere is usually involved in intellectual activities of sequencing, analyzing, and inferring logical relationships. The right hemisphere is more active in visual imagery, holistic interpretation, and integration.

While a good deal of the neuropsychological research is relatively new, the findings suggest that physical performance is affected by these different information-processing modes. Think about it. A complex act like hitting a golf ball requires both analysis and integration. We need to differentiate, analyze, and sequence the specific components of the swing; then we must integrate them into a single smooth behavior. Obviously, this is an act which requires more than half a brain! (There are days when we wonder if a whole brain is enough.)

In any case, golfers may be helped by thinking about the different ways we can process information. Most of us probably rely primarily on analysis. We read detailed reports of specifics of grip, stance, takeaway, and the like. This is where the notion of *information overload* comes in. We can only think clearly about so much at any moment.

The disruptive effects of information overload have been demonstrated in school classrooms, in psychological laboratories, and in our everyday living. We all remember times when we were overwhelmed by the amount of information with which we were faced. At a conference, you're introduced to many new people; then you can't remember their names—just too much new information to learn all at once. You go to the supermarket with a list in your head; the list is long, and you forget several crucial items. Psychologically, these "breakdowns" in information processing are to be expected. You tried to remember too much; your information-processing system was overloaded.

Enough, Already!

Information overload causes problems for golfers, especially for high-handicap golfers. We all have read, heard, or been taught so many things that we have trouble remembering what is important. How many times have you gone to the first tee (you're already tense) and tried to get set for the first shot? Running through your head are admonitions about grip, stance, ball position, setup, takeaway, shoulder turn, weight shift, and follow-through. If you're like most of us, this is too much information: Your system is overloaded. The consequence is increased tension and a breakdown in performance. Your drive is a disaster and your confidence takes a giant step backward.

How can you prevent information overload? The answer is to organize and to reduce the amount of information you try to deal with at any one time. As you set up for a shot, you cannot attend to the many instructions and suggestions you have read or heard. If you try to remember everything, you'll be hopelessly confused, and, as a consequence, your swing will come apart. Instead, you must learn to concentrate on a limited amount of information. You must reduce, simplify, and synthesize the information you process so you can execute the shot.

Don't Blow Your Fuse

Golfers use a variety of techniques to cut down information and to improve their performance. Whatever your particular strategy, when you are ready to start your swing, it is psychologically to your advantage to adopt a relatively simple and well-learned plan for action. Complete your review of the many bits of advice about stance, grip, and the like, then put them out of your mind. Reduce your information load. Instead of analyzing, let the integrative processes take over.

Here are some ways golfers use to integrate and smooth their swings: Some control and direct their actions by reminding themselves to "slow down the backswing." Others count a rhythmic "1, 2, 3, swing." Still others concentrate only on hitting the number on the ball.

Some golfers use imagery in guiding their swings. Imagery includes visualizing the flight of the ball, visualizing the way you look at the completion of your swing, or visualizing the club-ball impact. Although we usually refer to imagery as visual, there are many kinesthetic feelings in golf that add to the power of the visualization. What is important is the synthesis of what we see and feel. For some, this synthesis is enhanced through the use of imagery. Remember, though, it is difficult, if not impossible, to use visual-kinesthetic imagery while you are in the process of

analyzing the components of your shot. The analysis
comes first; then the integration takes over.

In trying to hit the ball better, most of us try to take too
much information into account. Remember that you can
process only so much information at a given time whether
you're at a business meeting, in a classroom, or on the golf
course. Tension and anxiety are consequences of information overload. High levels of tension and anxiety lead to
poor performance.

The Snark Is a Boojum?

Still another source of tension is uncertainty. Anxiety increases when we receive confusing, uncertain, or ambiguous instructions. Unfortunately, many women suffer a
great deal of confusion and uncertainty in many aspects of
the game. Consider the language of golf. We hear and read
about open stances, power grips, closed club face, hooking
lies, and on and on. Most of us have some vague notions
about what these terms mean, but we often find them confusing and ambiguous. Because we are unclear about their
meanings, we cannot integrate these ideas into our
information-processing systems, and so they, too, add to
our tensions.

How Was That Again?

Ambiguous information or terminology is even more anxiety arousing when it is coupled with confusing instructions. Like it or not, women golfers receive a great deal of instruction and advice from spouses, playing partners, friends, golf magazines, and television announcers. Too often this instruction is ambiguous, confusing, and sometimes even conflicting.

You've been told that for certain shots the ball should be moved forward. Does this mean further out in front of you or further to your left? One friend tells you to use a putting grip and stiff arm shot to run the ball onto the green from a short distance. In the same situation, a second friend advocates use of a sand wedge and a soft shot to the pin. Since you are uncertain about the better strategy, and not too sure how to do either, you are apt to tense up and blow whichever shot you choose.

Whether we are talking about grip, stance, club selection, or shot, the psychological principle is that ambiguous, confusing, or conflicting information leads to tension. Too much tension disrupts play.

Attention And Golf

We have already discussed the disruptive effect of too much anxiety or too little involvement. Another closely related source of disruption for golfers is distraction.

Some days you may feel relaxed and in control of your game. You are able to shut out extraneous sights and sounds and to ignore the idle chatter of your partners. On other days, you seem to be especially sensitive to the world around you. You respond to every comment of your playing companions; you hear every whisper on the tee. Your tension level rises and your golf swing goes to pieces.

Clang, Clang, Clang Goes the Trolley

Every round of golf is full of potential distractors which can disrupt your concentration and affect your ability to sustain attention. Psychologists have studied the effects of distractors on performance on a variety of tasks. Two of their findings are of special interest to golfers.

First, different things are distractors for different people. A playing partner's chatter may be very disruptive to one person but seemingly unimportant to another. A helicopter overhead will divert one putter's attention, yet be completely ignored by the others in the same foursome. Distractors are indeed in the eye and ear of the beholder.

Second, distractors that are disruptive in one situation may lead to increased concentration in others. Psychological research in the laboratory has shown that sometimes we perform better when there are lights flashing or bells ringing. Of course, when distractions are intense enough, everyone's concentration will be disrupted.

Think about it. On the golf course, your attention and concentration are usually upset by distractors which are relatively mild. It is your own inability to deal with these distractors and, therefore, your inability to control and to direct your attention that leads to problems in your play. We would like to blame a bad shot on the sound of the power mower or the bark of a dog. The truth of the matter is that most of our distractions are in our own heads. Although we are on the course, we are not there psychologically, and we are easily distracted by external and internal events.

When you are distracted, you lose control over your own game, you raise your level of anxiety, and you play poorly. Remember, performance is at its peak at the top of the upside-down U.

Who Can't Concentrate?

Another factor which influences golfers' performance is fatigue. Physical fatigue alone may disrupt your ability to attend and to concentrate. Fatigue may be a particularly potent factor if it's a hot day or if you're playing a billy-goat course with much walking up and down hill.

Physical fatigue is only one kind of fatigue, however. The effects of mental fatigue on performance are very powerful. You may be especially drained after an important match, when on other more relaxed days, you have easily managed 18 holes and still felt fresh.

Even on relaxed days, golf requires the ability to concentrate for several hours. Sustaining attention over long periods of time is not easy. Mental fatigue is a very real source of disruption which reduces performance and raises scores. Evidence from psychological research holds some important lessons for golfers.

It Only Seems Like Forever

Psychologists have demonstrated over and over again that the quality of our performance changes as we carry out an activity over a relatively long period of time. School children make more errors on simple arithmetic problems in the middle of an assignment than they do at the beginning, even though the problems are similar in level of difficulty. Adults are less accurate in radar screen monitoring after several hours of uninterrupted viewing than they are during the first hour.

Problems of maintaining attention over long periods of time may be shown graphically. The performance curve looks something like this:

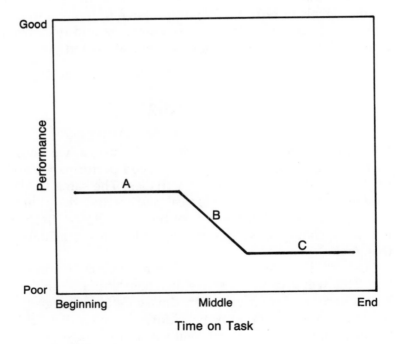

Note that performance is good at the beginning (Segment A) and is maintained for some time. Near the middle of the task (Segment B), there is a drop. Then performance levels out (Segment C). Mental fatigue increases and concentration decreases over time.

Achtung! Achtung!

What do laboratory studies of sustained attention have to do with mental fatigue in golf? Really quite a lot. Good golf demands attention, particularly the ability to sustain attention.

Consider these facts: It takes over 4 hours to complete an average round of golf. Few of us can maintain attention for 1 hour, let alone 4. It's not surprising that your concentration, your involvement, and your level of attention vary in different parts of the game. It doesn't make sense to expect to maintain the same level of concentration for 4 full hours. You must expect some ups and downs in your concentration and in your play.

Concentrating for long periods of time is tiring. It leads to high levels of tension. What you have to learn is to control and direct your attention, to disengage and relax from time to time, and to focus and concentrate when you need to.

Quo Vadis?

From the psychological research just discussed, we know that feeling in control leads to improved performance and to greater satisfaction in many activities. The same holds true in golf. From a psychological perspective, the golfer's goal is to increase her feelings of being in charge. In the following chapters, we describe specific ways to achieve this goal.

First, we'll show you how to compute your Personal Par. This will give you a sense of where you are now. You'll become a smarter golfer, devise better strategies, improve your attention, and cut down on your distractibility and fatigue; in short, you will learn to manage your energy.

5

Personal Par:
A Psychological
System For
Better Golf

If you are lucky enough to play golf once a week or more, you know that your performance varies from round to round. You may play to a good score on Tuesday morning and then have a disastrous round on Thursday. You may feel relaxed and confident one day and tense and unsure the next. These variations in performance cannot be explained by changes in the level of technical skill you bring to the game.

True, most golfers play at a limited level of technical skill, but that level doesn't change dramatically on a daily or weekly basis. What does vary is the level of psychological control over the game, and it is variations in psychological control which lead to the ups and downs of play.

Who's in Charge of Your Game?

From a psychological perspective, your most important accomplishment is to feel "in charge" of your game. Earlier, we discussed the notion of locus of control as an important motivational influence on how we play and on how much we enjoy the experience of golf. The who's-in-charge-of-your-game question is not only important in how you play, but it also affects your decisions about where you play, with whom you play, and the circumstances in which you play.

One Step at a Time

The first step to better psychological control of your golf involves goal setting. We have already spoken about the notion of flow—the experience of having everything come together so that your play is easy, smooth, and on target. This seemingly effortless performance is most apt to occur when your goals and your abilities are matched. We know that performance and satisfaction are greatest when we seek goals which stretch us a bit but which we have a chance of achieving. These goals lead to tension levels which are in the middle of the upside-down U. When we set our goals too high or too low, our performance deteriorates, and we get little satisfaction out of what we do.

Should I Play to Par?

If you analyze your own game and the games of your playing partners, you will realize that most of the time you set

goals which do not match your abilities. You often aspire
to scores that are not achievable. You start every round of
golf at a psychological disadvantage because there is little
likelihood that you can achieve your goals. The consequence is tension levels which are disruptive, along with
negative feelings of disappointment and frustration.

These feelings are not a necessary part of your game
whatever your level of skill. Through a process of self-
analysis, you can set levels of aspiration which lead to better play and which bring you more pleasure. The task is
not easy, but in a relatively brief period of time, it leads to
obvious improvement, making the game more fun. As a
start, let's look at the notion of par.

What is Par?

Referring specifically to golf, Webster says par is "the
number of strokes set as a standard for a hole or a complete course." Remember, par is an *arbitrary* standard
which varies somewhat according to course. Par is 72 at
Pebble Beach and 70 at Merion, both U.S. Open champion-
ship courses. Par also varies according to who is playing.
On the same course, the par for men may be 71 and the
par for women 74.

Arbitrary or not, however, par provides an external and
objective standard of performance. It may be viewed as a
common yardstick against which all players can be
measured. This view of par is useful for pros, low handicappers, and for those in serious competition, but it is a
standard which is beyond the reach of most golfers.

Give up the Gold Standard

For most of us, regulation par represents a level of performance which is unrealistic. When we set such a standard
as our goal, we have predetermined that we will fail. For
most golfers, the discrepancy between regulation par and
their own scores for a round will be between 20 and 40
strokes.

It is not surprising, then, that many times we finish a round feeling discouraged and frustrated. The harder we strive to achieve an unachievable goal, the more tense, anxious, and discouraged we become. For most golfers, par is an unachievable goal. In fact, accepting par as the only "real" standard of performance is not only unrealistic for most of us, but it may actually lower our performance and raise our scores.

How can we resolve the problem of the discrepancy between an unrealistic goal or standard and our actual ability to achieve it? Psychologically, the answer is clear. Most golfers need to play to a different definition of par.

We need to define goals which are realistic for us, goals which lead to better performance on the course. This means we should play to goals we control, not to goals determined by others. One way to achieve this is to redefine par using the notion of *Personal Par*.

What is Personal Par?

From a psychological perspective, Personal Par is best thought of as a personal standard. It is the arbitrary number of strokes that each golfer sets for herself to complete a round. The "official" value of par for a given course may be 72. For one golfer, Personal Par may be 80; for another, Personal Par may be 102; for a third golfer, it may be 116. In fact, the higher your average score, the more important the idea of Personal Par.

Remember, the value of Personal Par is relative, not absolute. It is negotiable and individual. Change it as your skills change. Whatever the value of regulation or official par, make your goal for each round to play to your own standard, to match or break your own Personal Par.

Personal Par is a specific goal for each hole. We can illustrate with holes from a course familiar to us. For instance, on our home course, the official par for hole #13 is 4. At 350 yards, the 13th hole is the number two handicap hole for women on this course. The golfer faces a long, steep, uphill approach to an elevated green which is protected by a large and very deep bunker. To add to the

HOLE #13
350 YARDS
PAR 4

problems, the driving area slopes sharply to the right, running away from the green. Many well-hit drives have skittered down hill, making the hole play extra long.

Given the length and difficulty of this hole, it is the rare woman golfer who can reach the green in two shots. Yet, the official or regulation par is 4. For most golfers, however, Personal Pars should be 5, 6, or 7 on this hole. It is as much of an accomplishment for a high handicapper to get on the green in 4 and to make her par of 6 as it is for a scratch golfer to get on in 2 and make her par of 4. A personal birdie 5 is to be celebrated with as much enthusiasm as a regulation birdie 3.

Personal Par is also well-illustrated by the 17th hole on our home course. This is a 193-yard official par 3. The green is bunkered on both sides and rises sharply to a ridge covered with heavy rough. There is a deep swale immediately in front of the green. The fairway runs slightly to the right so that any ball hit to that side is likely to end up in the adjacent fairway.

For 9 out of 10 women golfers, Personal Par on this hole is 4 because it takes most women two shots to reach the green. Yet, too often, a well-played 4 is interpreted as a failure because the golfer has bought into an unrealistic standard of 3.

Recognize that par is a relative value and you free yourself from competing against an arbitrary, external, and frequently meaningless standard. Fortunately, golf is an individual game which allows you to play against yourself. *Your real goal is to match or better your own Personal Par.*

HOLE #17
193 YARDS
PAR 3

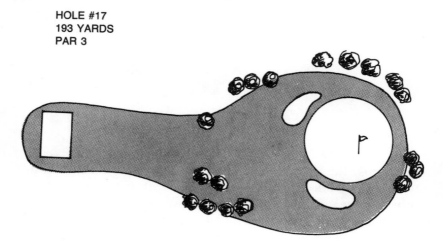

How To Compute Your Personal Par

The way to compute your Personal Par for a given period, and a given course, is to analyze your recently played rounds.

Note that Personal Par, like regulation par, is computed on the assumption that you will take two putts on every green. Alas, most of us don't always manage to get down in two, but we balance the score with occasional one-putts. For most of us, an average of two putts is a reasonable goal.

The Big Difference is Tee to Green

If most golfers average two putts a hole, then how can we explain the broad differences in total scores recorded after any hole or any round? Differences among scores are explained mostly in the number of strokes necessary to get from tee to green. For a long hitter, the tee-to-green strokes may be 2. The short hitter may take 4 to cover the same distance. For the first golfer, the value of Personal Par for the hole is 4; for the second golfer, the Personal Par for the same hole is 6.

As you compute your own Personal Par, you'll see that the values of Personal Par differ on a hole-by-hole basis as well as on a person-by-person basis. Because Personal Pars are computed allowing two putts per hole, the size of the par varies according to the number of strokes you average from tee to green.

Notice, though, that distance is not the only thing that affects the number of tee-to-green strokes. Two holes of similar length may require different numbers of tee-to-green strokes for the same golfer. In the case of a flat, wide, trouble-free fairway, a golfer may reasonably expect to be on the green in 2. In the case of an uphill fairway and a well-trapped, elevated green, the same golfer may require 3 shots. So the values of par would be 4 and 5 for the two holes respectively.

Personal Par is determined according to how you play each hole, not just the distances listed on the score card. Personal Par reflects how you actually play, not how you *should, could, might,* or *ought* to play. Personal Par provides you with a hole-by-hole analysis of your current level of golfing performance.

Here's How

To get started you will need the hole-by-hole scores for your latest four rounds on your home course. Now tear out a worksheet from the back of the book and follow along with us.

Step 1

On the first line of the worksheet, enter the date round one was played and the tee-to-green strokes that you scored for each hole on that day. If you didn't keep track of your putts, assume that you took the regulation 2 per hole—and from now on, record your putts as you play.

Step 2

On the next lines, record the dates and scores for rounds two, three, and four the same way. Fill in the tee-to-green strokes for each hole.

Step 3

Now total these tee-to-green strokes for each hole and average the scores. The average will rarely be a whole number, so round up to the next higher number when the decimal value is .5 or more. If the decimal is .4 or less, round down. Record the average rounded score for each hole.

Step 4

Add two strokes on each hole for putts and write this grand total at the bottom. The total is your Personal Par for each hole on the course.

True Confessions

Look at the illustration to see how the system works. Carol's scores for four rounds are on the left and are recorded by date. On the first hole, her tee-to-green scores were 4, 5, 4, and 6—that's a total of 19 to be divided by 4. Since the result of this arithmetic is 4.75, she rounded up to 5. Carol expects to reach the green in 5 strokes. Add 2 putts. Carol's Personal Par for hole #1 is 7. So 7 is entered at the bottom of the column for the first hole.

DATE / HOLE	1	2	3	4	16	17	18
APRIL 17	4	3	2	6	6	3	5
APRIL 24	5	3	1	4	5	2	4
MAY 1	4	4	3	5	5	2	4
MAY 8	6	3	2	6	21	9	17
TOTAL	19	13	8		5	2	4
AVERAGE	5	3	2		+2	+2	+2
PUTTS	+2	+2	+2		7	4	6
PERSONAL PAR	7	5	4				

Carol's Personal Par

As you can see, every hole is a different story. On the second hole, Carol reached the green in 3, 3, 4, and 3. The total of 13 was divided by 4, giving an average score of 3.25. Rounding the decimal down, Carol recorded an average of 3 tee-to-green strokes for this hole. She then added 2 putts. Her Personal Par for the second hole is 5.

On hole #3, a regulation par 3, Carol recorded 2, 1, 3, and 2 tee-to-green shots. This totals 8, and when divided by 4 shows that Carol averaged 2 shots to the green on this hole. Add 2 putts and her Personal Par is 4 for the third hole.

While different from the regulation pars for these holes, Carol's Personal Pars set a challenging but realistic goal for her at her present level of play. As her game changes, she must reset the values of her Personal Pars.

Remember that Personal Par is relative, not absolute. The numerical value will be different for different golfers and will differ for each of us at various times. Personal and situational factors will affect the value of Personal Par. Both need to be taken into account when computing your pars.

If you take a 3 month winter golf break, your Personal Pars will probably be higher in early spring than in late summer or fall. If you play a good many rounds in unusually heavy weather, you may have to modify your pars temporarily. The values of your Personal Pars will be higher if you are recovering from a back injury or as you get older and lose flexibility. You may also need to consider some adjustment in Personal Pars to fit the particular course you are playing. Personal Pars represent your realistic and current golfing goals, not someone else's. From a psychological perspective, the values of Personal Pars represent optimal levels of challenge for you.

Just Another Handicapping System?

Golfers who have official handicaps will recognize that the idea of Personal Par is similar to a handicapping system. But there are several important differences between Personal Par and most other handicapping systems. Psychologically these differences are important.

First, remember that official handicaps are computed on total scores for 18 holes. As we illustrated in the last section, Personal Par is computed separately for each hole. The psychological effect of Personal Par on a hole-by-hole basis is to provide short-term and specific goals, to enhance attention to the play on each hole, and to minimize the tendency to remember a failure on previous holes. Playing to Personal Par on a hole-by-hole basis increases your attention and your likelihood of success.

Remember, too, that official handicaps are computed so that golfers can play against one another. The purpose of handicapping is to equalize differences in ability so that golfers with different skills can compete. But competition is only one of the many reasons women play golf. For most of us, the enjoyment of the game is in the playing, not in the competition. In fact, except for a few local club tournaments, most of us compete with ourselves rather than with our playing partners. Our goal is to lower our own scores, not to beat someone else's. Personal Par, as its name suggests, is an individual standard. It provides realistic goals which reflect individual good play. Personal Par is not a way to equalize competition.

A third difference between a handicap system and Personal Par is how they are computed. Handicaps are usually computed using the 10 best scores the golfer has posted in her last 20 rounds. The value of the handicap represents the optimal score over those rounds. It does not represent the average score for those rounds. Because the size of the handicap represents the optimal level of play, it is frequently inconsistent with the golfer's current level of play. The size of the handicap seldom represents the actual score of the once-a-week golfer.

Remember our discussion about the psychological impact of goals which are discrepant from our ability? It is not surprising that you feel frustrated when you set your handicap as your goal. Psychologically, you will do better to play to your Personal Par on a hole-by-hole basis.

Finally, and perhaps most important psychologically, the difference between Personal Par and most handicapping systems is that Personal Par is under your control. It is not determined by an unknown computer. Because you compute the value of Personal Par, you can adjust it for each hole. You can account for regular play or can allow for extended periods of nonplay. The value of Personal Par for each hole becomes your immediate and realistic goal. Playing to Personal Par means being in charge of your game. Being in charge of your game means setting your own Personal Pars.

Some Benefits Of Playing To Personal Par

A hole-by-hole analysis of your play on your home course will provide you with a detailed and differentiated analysis of your current golfing abilities. Furthermore, it will lead to insights about your game that will improve your play. You will also end up with a record of where and how your game has improved.

Because you set your own Personal Pars relative to your game, you can modify them as your game changes. As we noted earlier, goals which are too discrepant from ability lead to disappointment and frustration, or to boredom and lack of concentration or effort. It would be self-defeating for a golfer who averages rounds of 115 to set a goal of shooting a 95. Yet a 95 might be a goal which increases the motivation and concentration of the golfer who plays to a usual 100. The golfer who averages 115 may play better and more wisely when she realizes her Personal Par is 112. A lower handicap golfer who plays regularly may set a Personal Par of 90 but might have to reset the goal to 95 after a year away from golf.

We can begin with our own golfing experiences. Carol's handicap is 30; her scores vary between 100 and 115. Carol's goal is to reduce her Personal Par from 109 to 105. Barbara's handicap is 18; her scores range from 89 to 94. Carol wants to ''break 100'' one of these days. Barbara wants to ''break 85'' soon! During the next month, Carol's

goal might be to average 104; the comparable goal for Barbara is to play consistently under 90. During the second month, the goals may be modified to 102 for Carol, 88 for Barbara. Although the actual values of the goals differ, both golfers improve their games and increase their feelings of accomplishment when they play to their Personal Pars.

Just as golfers differ in their individual goals, so will the goals for a given golfer vary at different times. The goals for each round will be influenced by the course to be played, the weather on that day, and the amount of play the golfer has been able to get in the preceding weeks. The psychological point to remember is that the most optimal goals are those which are set according to your past performance. You play best when goals are demanding but attainable.

Who Needs Dr. Freud?

In addition to setting psychologically positive goals, the hole-by-hole analysis of Personal Par is useful in calling at tention to areas of strength and weakness within your game. It also will help set realistic expectancies for each shot. For example, a short hitter may realize that she averages 2 over the official par 5 on very long holes. She never reaches the green in 3, but must regularly count on 5 to get there. Her Personal Par is 7, not the regulation 5. Our short hitter may find, too, that on some of the medium-length holes (most of which are official par 4s), she cannot reach the green even with three good shots. So, for those holes, her par must be 6. On other medium-length holes, this golfer may be able to reach the green in 3; thus, the value of her Personal Par should be set at 5.

Remember too, small increments of change which test us and attract us are powerful motivators. Each golfer must determine the most optimal goals for herself.

Goals and aspirations must be viewed as personal, relative, and changeable. In a system of Personal Par, you set them for each hole, each round, and for longer time periods. From a psychological perspective, Personal Par means positive goal setting and represents levels of aspiration which will maximize your performance.

What's So Hard About Personal Par?

Playing to realistic goals as exemplified by the system of Personal Par is psychologically difficult to accept for one important reason: It forces you to accept your own game, to acknowledge your own limitations. This can be a painful process most of us seek to avoid.

All of us like to remember the one time we got on the green of a long par 4 in 2 shots, ignoring many rounds that we took 3 or even 4 strokes to get there. We like to recall the time we made a long side-hill putt to save a par 3 on a short hole, or the day we chipped in for a birdie. These shots are great fun and provide satisfying memories. They do not reflect our usual game, however. It is unrealistic to think that we *can* play at that level regularly, or that we *ought* to play at that level regularly.

Psychologists have demonstrated over and over again that performance in most activities is influenced by our views of what we think we should be able to do as well as

what we actually can do. Golf is difficult enough without the additional psychological burden of unrealistic expectations. Establishing Personal Par on a hole-by-hole basis provides you with a solid understanding of your own game.

Get Smart!

We have already suggested that adopting Personal Par as the standard for play will reduce tension and anxiety which develop when we aspire to unrealistic goals or when we set our expectancies too high. On a hole-by-hole basis, the goal of Personal Par also leads to improved planning and to better golf strategies.

In addition to being less tense, you will make wiser and more realistic decisions about club choice, type of shot, and how much risk to take. Instead of having to get every inch out of every shot in order to reach the green of a regulation par 4 hole in 2, you can play a second shot to get into good position to come onto the green in 3. This will almost assure two putts for your Personal Par and will occasionally get you a personal birdie with a one-putt.

Expectations, strategies, and tensions go together and can help or hurt your game. How many times have you ended up in a sand trap or in the rough or muffed a shot because you had to get onto a green in one shot for a chance at making regulation par? How many times have you topped a ball or hit it fat because you had to make up for a previously badly hit ball? For most golfers, attempting to play to an unrealistic standard leads to poor decisions and to bad shots. Playing to your Personal Par will not only make the game more fun, but it will improve your playing strategy, help you know your game better, and take strokes off your score.

To Err is Human

For many of us, a round of golf might be described as a comedy of errors. Golfers are very human. We hit almost as many poor shots as good ones. And our bad shots are sometimes quite remarkable! (Sometimes the ball seems to have a life of its own.) Personal Par gives a better understanding of your game, including the kinds of mistakes you make.

Be aware of three types of errors: those that are a result of poor judgment, those that are caused by poor execution, and those that occur because of lack of skill. All three types occur often if you don't know your own game, if you haven't paid attention to the situation. You may think you can hit farther than you can, so you select a 9 iron instead of an 8 or even a 7. That's an error in judgment and usually adds at least 1 stroke to your score. However, even if you have selected the right club, you may execute badly so that the ball is not hit well. If the shot is one you can hit, then practice will make you more consistent, and you will save strokes. On the other hand, it takes a great deal more than practice to hit the kind of shots that the professional golfers do so well on television. Regardless of how much practice, few of us can hit the ball 225 yards or can put spin on a ball to pull it back to the cup. We are doomed to failure if we attempt these shots. It's foolish to blame yourself for a bad shot if the shot is beyond your ability; no matter how hard you try, you are not going to manage it. By analyzing your game within your Personal Par, you can understand and control the kinds of errors which plague your game. You can play smarter and better golf.

Some different playing strategies based on different Personal Pars are illustrated here. We have diagrammed the playing strategies of three hypothetical players, Ace, Barbara, and Carol. Ace plays to an overall official handicap of 10, Barbara to an 18, and Carol to a 30.

Look at the first diagram. It shows the 13th hole on our home course. We have already described #13—an extremely difficult, long, and uphill hole. The regulation par is 4, yet there are only a few women golfers who can realistically expect to reach this green in 2. Even a well-hit second shot often ends up in the trap by the green. Barbara and Carol, middle and high handicappers, play to Personal Pars of 5 and 6 on this hole.

As you look at the diagram, it is obvious that high handicapper Carol has a much easier shot to the green than Barbara does, and Ace has the most difficult shot of all. For Barbara and Carol, the strategy is not to hit the ball as far as they can, but rather to get the ball into position to come to the green close to the pin.

HOLE #13
350 YARDS
PAR 4

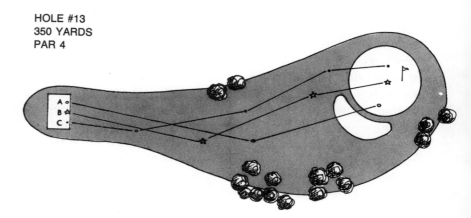

HOLE #2
326 YARDS
PAR 4

The second hole on our home course is a 326-yard par 4 with out-of-bounds to the left and fairway traps and trees to the right. A narrow but deep green is slightly elevated and well trapped on both the right and left as well as at the back. There is a narrow opening in the center leading into the heart of the green, but a swale with deep rough runs across the fairway slightly in front of the opening. The drawing shows the layout of this hole and the strategies our three different golfers took to get on the green. Our drawing shows how all three get on the green to make their Personal Pars.

As you can see from the diagram, from length alone it is possible for a long hitter to get on the green in 2. That's golfer Ace. However, more times than not, those long shots end up in the well-placed traps or in the rough. This is a precision hole which rewards accuracy as much as distance.

The low handicap big hitter, Ace, has to hit two good wood shots or a wood and a long iron to reach the green in 2. As you can see from the placement of the traps and trees, this means two accurate and difficult shots.

In contrast, middle and high handicappers Barbara and Carol, whose Personal Pars are 5 or even 6, are able to play for position so that they can come onto the green without trouble. Notice, too, that although golfers Barbara and Carol may have different size handicaps, they both are likely to be on the green in 3. Looking at the realistic expectancies for the Personal Par 5 and 6 golfers, it is clear that they have easier shots to the green than the big hit-

HOLE #17
193 YARDS
PAR 3

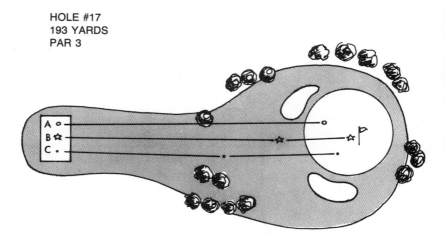

ters. Their chances of making their Personal Pars are good. For the shorter hitters who have set higher Personal Pars, this hole is a potential birdie. For the golfer who must get on the green with two long shots, it is a potential bogie.

Look at the diagrams of two regulation par 3s. With a well-hit shot on hole #17, Ace can reach the green in 1. Her Personal Par is 3. For Barbara, the hole consistently requires a wood and a pitching wedge; for Carol a wood and a 7 iron. For both Barbara and Carol, Personal Par is 4. Note how much easier it is for Barbara and Carol to make their Personal Pars than it is for Ace to make hers.

Now look at a diagram of the third hole on our home course. This is a regulation par 3, 108-yard hole with a steeply elevated green trapped on both left and right sides. Middle and low handicap golfers can reasonably expect to reach the green in 1 from the tee, but high handicapper Carol requires a tee shot and an iron. Notice, that for Carol the second shot to the green is a short one. She often can get the ball close to the pin and putt for her birdie. In contrast, the two other golfers must get by traps, yet keep the ball on the green. For the middle handicapper Barbara, this is an especially difficult hole as it requires distance, height, and accuracy from the tee.

Also notice that on the third hole Barbara and Ace played to the same Personal Pars (3). On the second hole, Barbara and Carol played to the same Personal Par (5).

HOLE #3
108 YARDS
PAR 3

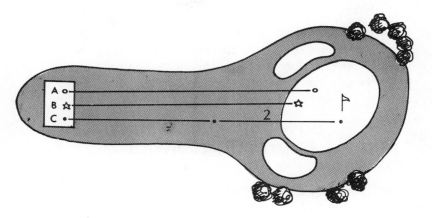

What you must remember is that par is relative, that it varies according to the golfer and to the hole.

Every Story Has a Moral

Setting hole-by-hole Personal Pars helps you work out playing strategies, taking into account your own skill level and the particular characteristics of the hole to be played. When you look carefully at the layouts of most golf courses, you can see that most of the trouble is around the green. There the traps are placed to snare even slightly er- rant balls. The rough is at its thickest, and if there is water, it is close. Thinking that we ought to play to the magical goal of the regulation par, many of us find ourselves straining to hit the ball hard in order to get every inch, forgetting the character of the hole itself. The unfortunate and frequent consequence is a ball in the trap, rough, or water.

The moral of this story is that successful golf requires realistic strategies for playing. For the low handicapper on a particular hole, this may mean attempting to hit two good woods to get on the green in 2; for the middle handi- capper, it may mean planning to get on with two woods and a short iron; for the high handicapper, it may mean playing two woods and two irons, or three woods and a short iron. For you, it means planning strategies that fit your own game; it means playing within yourself.

By playing to Personal Par, you can concentrate on accuracy, not just distance. You can adopt strategies in which you play for position, and because you position your shots well, you cut down on trouble. You also score better.

How Can Personal Par Improve Attention?

When you play golf, you are faced with many demands on your attention. The demands vary according to what you hope to accomplish and to the conditions in which you are playing. Golf requires that you attend to a whole range of information, that you read the relevant cues, that you integrate the information into some plan for action, and that you make decisions about how to carry out the plan.

Imagine that you are getting ready to hit your third shot to a par 4 green. At the very least, you must be aware of the distance between the ball and the green, observe whether the green is elevated or low, consider the location of sand traps or water, and note the pin position relative to the size and shape of the green. You also need to take into account the depth of the rough, the amount and direction of the wind, and the likelihood that the green is hard and dry or soft and wet. If it is your home course, you probably review local knowledge about which direction the ball runs on this hole. We have already discussed the importance of taking situational factors into account when computing your Personal Pars. The process of computing and checking your Personal Pars will also draw attention to the situational factors which affect your play.

Questions, Questions, Questions!

As if all this weren't complicated enough, you also must be aware of your own abilities and must determine how they match the demands of the shot. Should you use a soft 7 wood or a firm 5 or 6 iron? Are you better at high soft shots aimed directly at the pin, or do you play a pitch-and-run shot more effectively? Can you hit the ball the necessary distance with confidence, or should you lay up and play for a shorter more accurate shot? Are you hot and tired or cool and fresh?

Clearly the demands on your attention are real, even for relatively uncomplicated shots. To add to your problems further, you must concentrate for the full time it takes to complete a round. No wonder you are tired after play, and no wonder you have problems in concentration and in sustaining attention.

Listening to golfers talk about a just completed round underscores how important attention is in the game. "I lost my concentration" or "I couldn't keep my mind on the game" are common explanations for bad rounds. "I was really into my game" or "I had my rhythm" are common descriptions of how the golfer felt as she played a good round. Whether describing good or poor performance, the golfer was talking about attention.

It's Called Daydreaming

We have already discussed how attention affects performance in the psychological laboratories and in the classrooms. The same principles hold on the golf course. We perform best when we attend well. Maintaining attention over a 4- to 5-hour period is extremely difficult, and most golfers cannot do it. Few of us can control, focus, and direct our attention exclusively on golf throughout a whole round. Yet we know the level of our play deteriorates as we let our minds wander off to think of other things.

How can you solve the problem of paying attention to golf for the time it takes to complete a round? The answer is to shorten the demands on your concentration. It is here that the notion of Personal Par becomes important.

Divide and Conquer

One of the benefits of playing to a hole-by-hole Personal Par is that you control and reduce demands on sustaining attention and concentration. In effect, you break up the course into 18 separate units. Each unit has a specific goal (Personal Par) and each is played as if it stands alone. Viewed this way, you have to maintain concentration only for a matter of 10 to 15 minutes at a time. In other words, you have to attend only long enough to play one hole. You don't have to maintain uninterrupted attention for the total time you are on the golf course.

Think of attending on the golf course as cyclical—intense concentration while playing a hole, less involvement and lowered attention between holes. If you think of attending in this way, you see that the demands on your concentration vary according to the length of time it takes to play 1 hole, not the full 18.

The same logic holds on a shot-by-shot basis. By the very nature of golf, your concentration is broken up into a series of strokes. What you have to learn is to focus your attention at the time of the shot and to relax your attention between shots. Too often, you step up to the ball while still in the middle of a sentence. It's not surprising that you don't connect if you are still completing a story about your relatives' weekend visit or the plot of last night's TV show. The time to talk and visit is between shots; the time to concentrate is immediately before and during your shot.

Sports psychologists have found that establishing a regular preshot routine helps golfers to focus and to concentrate. In one study, for example, beginning golfers were encouraged to concentrate when they took the club out of the bag, not before. As part of the preshot attentional training, they were also encouraged to review mentally a checklist of technical points and to use imagery to visualize and feel what they wanted to do. This routine was effective in increasing attention, in focusing the golfers' efforts. For all of us, the establishment of a preshot routine will free up attention between shots, focus attention on the shot and, thus, improve play and reduce fatigue.

Demand and Supply

Some holes are harder than others. On our home course, the first hole is uphill and difficult, the third much less demanding. The 16th hole is long and treacherous, the 11th shorter and easier. It takes longer concentration to complete the 1st and the 16th holes than it does to complete the 3rd and 11th. Each hole requires your full attention during the time it is being played. But, because Personal Par is a separate goal for each hole, the demands on attention are limited.

Note, too, that attentional demands of a hole are not limited just to the length of the hole or to the time it takes to play it. Your concentration also is affected by psychological tensions. You may be more anxious on a tournament day than on a regular round, and your concentration may be affected. But remember, you perform best when your tensions are in the middle of the upside-down U. That's when your concentration is the best, too.

Psychologically, attention is one of the important facets of learning and performance. For golfers, attention is essential. It helps us gather information on which to make decisions about shots and clubs. Yet we all know that sustaining attention for long periods of time is difficult if not impossible. Personal Par enhances attention by breaking up the course into 18 separate units. It provides optimal motivational levels and regulates tension. It also improves your play.

In earlier parts of this book, we described how motivation, tension, and mental fatigue affect your play. Now we have also shown how you can improve your game through a system of Personal Par. In the following chapters, we focus on the psychological management of yourself as a golfer.

Managing Yourself On The Course

Course management is one of those exotic but ambiguous terms in the golfing lexicon. It is usually heard when a golfer advantageously plays the contours of a fairway to get the most out of a mediocre drive or threads a ball between two trees and gets a lucky bounce off a large boulder onto the green. While the term has a nice ring, from a psychological perspective, something far more important for the golfer to learn might be called *managing yourself on the course.*

Managing yourself does not mean improved techniques nor changes in technical skills. It does mean using your abilities to the maximum by controlling and directing your intellect and emotions.

We have already argued that psychological management is what golf is all about. This means being in control of yourself, shutting out distractions, focusing attention, and coordinating your mind and body. Golfers who manage themselves well direct their tensions and psychological energies in positive ways. The result is better play, lower scores, and more fun.

From psychological studies conducted in experimental laboratories and in clinics, we know that self-management applies to many human activities. It is likely that we would all be more efficient at work and less harried at home if we were better self-managers. This is particularly important in

golf, especially for women golfers who often feel uncertain, even overwhelmed, by the complexities of golf techniques. But remember, self-management is in the mind. A psychological approach to golf will increase self-management and improve play. Here are some specifics to consider.

Are You Ready to Play?

Managing yourself is not limited to the time you are actually on the golf course. It begins before you start to play. Unfortunately, many golfers are not ready to play at the beginning of a round. They are still in their other worlds—continuing a conversation with husband or child, planning the errands to be done when golf is over, thinking about a myriad of office chores left undone.

We have only to examine scores of holes played early on in a round to see that most golfers don't play them well. There are usually dubbed shots, poor choices of clubs, and half-hearted swings. Golfers often write off the "first-hole blues" as due to muscle stiffness or lack of warm-up.

We suggest that poor performance is often due to lack of psychological readiness to play. Our thoughts and minds are somewhere else—at the office or at home—when we

approach those first holes. It should not surprise us that
we do not play them well.

Who's Excited?

Does this scenario sound familiar? Tee time is 9:10. You arrive in the parking lot at 9:04, having rushed your family
through breakfast and out of the house, thrown on your
clothes, and driven the 3 miles to the golf course too fast.
In the parking lot, you kick off your sneakers, get into
your golf shoes, grab your bag and hat, lock the car, and
race to the starter's window, clutching your money, equip-
ment, and car keys. You arrive breathlessly on the tee at
9:10 with your shoes untied and your mind in a dither.
Psychologically ready for golf? No way.

Another familiar sequence goes like this: You arrive for
your 9:10 tee time half an hour early and meet your friends
in the coffee shop. The coffee is good, the surroundings
warm and comfortable, and the conversation interesting.
Suddenly it is 9:05, and the starter announces that you are
next off. You settle the coffee bill, gather your golf gear,
and hurry out to the first tee. You take two quick practice
swings to prepare for your first drive, still thinking about
your friend's marital problems or the plot of a new movie.
Psychologically ready for golf? No way.

Good golf depends on your psychological readiness for
play. Even though golf is usually played with other people, it is an individual game. Unlike team sports, you cannot depend on someone else to make your shots or decide
your strategies. Each golfer plays alone. The more ready
you are psychologically, the more you are apt to play well.

How Can I Get Psychologically Ready?

Getting ready to play means thinking about golf before
standing on the first tee. It means getting yourself psychologically focused on golf. It means disengaging from other
demands and interests. It's not always easy to accomplish,
but it's an important first step to good play. Here are some
practical suggestions:

Plan your schedule so that you have some time alone to think about golf before starting your round. You can't think about your game while you are rushing around trying to do too much in too little time. One practical strategy is to allow extra time to get ready. This may mean getting up half an hour earlier or preparing a simpler breakfast. It may mean setting a later start time. It may mean allowing a bit more time to drive to the course. You need time to get yourself together, to put some psychological as well as actual distance between you and your other worlds.

Once at the course, plan some time alone. The putting green is a good place for this. Few women golfers take advantage of the putting green. They think of it only as a place to improve their putting stroke. True, time on the putting green gives you a chance to get the feel of your stroke and to become attuned to the heaviness of the grass and air. More importantly, time on the putting green gives you time to think about play. A few minutes on the putting green provides a chance to gear up psychologically.

Be a Creature of Habit

Many golfers report that following a set routine also helps get them ready to play. Some take 6 putts from 2, then 4, then 8 feet. Others stay at the same distance from the hole until sinking 6 in a row. On the tee, some golfers go through a short exercise regimen, bending and twisting. Others may find that a sequence of practice swings with a long iron, then a 3-wood, and then a driver helps them to begin to concentrate on golf.

Each golfer must develop her own particular strategy or pregame warm-up. The important psychological principle to remember is that you will play better when you are comfortable, when you are in a familiar situation, and when you reduce uncertainty. Familiarity is increased when you think about your game ahead of time and when you go through a regular pregame routine or regimen. Anxiety is reduced, attention is focused, and concentration is increased as you get into your game. Getting ready to play is an important aspect of the game and should be viewed as part of managing yourself on the course.

How Do You Manage the Mechanics?

When we hear the phrase the mechanics of golf, most of us think of techniques of swing, stance, follow-through, and the like. These are the technical aspects of golf which are the province of the teaching pro. From the psychological perspective, we must also be concerned with the *mechanics of play*, as these are powerful influences on how we manage our games and on how successfully we play.

The golfer who has mastered the mechanics of play can devote her thoughts and energies to getting the ball into the cup. Inattention to the mechanics of play leads to hurry, confusion, tension, increased anxiety, and poor performance. Remember, performance is disrupted when our tensions get too far over on the upside-down U.

What Are the Mechanics of Play?

What do we mean by the mechanics of play? In the broadest sense, we mean being in the right place at the right time. The golfer who knows the mechanics of play is ready when it's her turn to hit, marks her ball on the green without having to be asked, tends the pin if closest to the hole, and leaves her cart or clubs on the side of the green nearest the next hole. In other words, she knows where she is on the course and where she is in her game. As a consequence, she does not have to hurry, has time to plan her shots, and does not have to deal with the frustration of catch-up golf. She has time to think about her game.

Life in the Trenches

Can you recall playing with a golfer who has not mastered the mechanics of play? The scenes go something like this:

Reminded on the first tee that it is her turn to drive, she put on her glove and looked for her tee and ball. On the third green, she had to be asked to mark her ball which was in a direct line with the golfer who stood ready to putt. As the last putter on the fourth hole, she forgot to put the pin back in the hole, and another member of the foursome went back to take care of it. On each hole she left her clubs well in front of the green, so she always had to trot back to get them. When holed out, she stood by the pin and counted her strokes.

Meanwhile, her companions grew more and more frustrated, play was slow, and by the fourth hole, the next foursome had to wait on every shot. Our golfer hurried faster and faster, almost running between shots. She was always behind. The result was increased tension, frustration, bad golf, and decreased enjoyment for everyone.

Attending to the mechanics of play helps you manage yourself and your game. It reduces the need for hurry, allows time for thinking through possible strategies for the next shot, and cuts down on the needless expenditure of energy involved in trying to catch-up. It also makes the game more enjoyable for you, your playing partners, and the golfers who follow.

Get Organized and Get With It

We have discussed the importance of getting into a psychological set of being ready to play. Mastering the mechanics of play reduces anxiety associated with hurry and stress and frees up your energies so that you may attend to playing well. From a psychological perspective, mastery of the mechanics of golf frees you to play.

We have shown throughout this book that the way to better and more satisfying golf is psychological control. Your control over your game shows in many ways. Golfers who manage themselves well set realistic but demanding goals. They attempt to play to their Personal Pars. They also come to the course ready to play. They attend to important cues which give them helpful information about the course and the specific playing conditions for the day. They are aware of where they are on the course and what comes next. They have learned to direct and sustain their energy and attention through a long round. In short, they feel comfortable with themselves. Psychologically, they are ready to play.

Choosing A Pro

All golfers profit from good instruction. Notice how many times you read that a big-name touring pro has spent a few days getting pointers from his mentor, or that two of the pros worked together to correct mistakes after a bad competitive round? There is so much to learn about golf that even expert players take lessons.

Help!

We all need help sometimes. Your game may change without your even being aware of it until you find you are in trouble. Things may fall apart, piece by piece, or sometimes all at once. You respond by tinkering here and there. You change your grip a bit, stand up straighter, shorten your backswing. Two months ago your swing was grooved, your game in place, and your confidence high. Suddenly, you find your game is gone, and you need help. That's a job for a professional teacher. The problem is to find the right teacher for you, and that's not always easy to do.

Psychologists who study how teachers teach and pupils learn have a difficult time defining what makes for good teaching. There isn't a single pattern of teaching that is the best. The important thing seems to be the ''match'' between the teacher and the pupil.

From classroom studies, we know that some children learn quickly and effectively when they work with teachers who are autocratic, directive, demanding, and focused on the task to be learned. Other children find these teachers cold and unresponsive; they learn better when their teachers are nondirective, low-key, relaxed, and more people-oriented. Both teachers may know their material and teach well, but their styles are effective with different kinds of pupils.

Pupils' and teachers' styles may match or conflict, and the result is success or failure in learning. Whether in the classroom or on the golf course, the match between pupil and teacher is an important determiner of the success of lessons. You must find a professional teacher who can work effectively with you—one who matches your style.

Where Do I Begin?

There are hundreds of teaching professionals who are members of the PGA or LPGA. These pros come in many sizes, shapes, ages, and colors, but have in common their enthusiasm for golf and considerable technical expertise. Many teaching professionals are young men and women who have aspirations to become touring pros. They are active, healthy, and strong with great balance and muscle tone; their eye-hand coordination is marvelous and their waists are slim. They turn clear through their backswing, hit the ball a mile, and play 18 holes without breathing heavily. They know a great deal about golf and how to play it. Let's face it—duffers don't become golf professionals.

The important question you must ask yourself is: "Will this pro be a good teacher for me?" It is just not a question of the pro being a good teacher or a bad teacher. Neither is it a question of whether you are a good learner or a poor learner. The point to consider is whether the pro is the right match for you.

Is This a Good Pro for Me?

How do you know if you and your pro are a good match? Perhaps the most important thing is that you are comfortable with your pro. Comfortable is a funny word—imprecise and hard to define—yet we all know when we feel comfortable with someone and when we don't. Think about it. When you feel comfortable with a person, you feel relaxed, you can take a few risks, you can fail without feeling rejected or put down, and you know that you are valued for what you are.

Whatever the level of your game, whether you are a 3 or a 30 handicapper, find a pro with whom you feel comfortable; it's the first step toward good instruction. Then what does it mean to feel comfortable psychologically?

Do You Agree on Goals?

First, you need a pro who accepts your aspirations, who understands where you are and where you want to be. We have already shown some of the effects of large discrepancies between goals and performance: lack of optimal attending and arousal, lowered motivation and effort, inconsistent play, and deteriorating performance—all are discouraging outcomes for both student and teacher. Both student and pro may be hardworking, motivated to improve, and competent: The problem may be in the match.

Two Scenarios

You have decided you have time to improve the worst parts of your game, especially your fairway woods and your long irons. Your pro has a different goal. The pro wants to redo your whole game and so outlines a plan for a year's overhaul. That's great if you have time, money, energy, and commitment to this long course of instruction. You're flattered that the pro thinks you have the potential of being that good, given the usual level of your game. However, club champion may not be your goal, and to set up a course of instruction that is demanding and long-term may be absolutely impossible for you to pull off.

The goals are discrepant, and both you and your pro are apt to be frustrated and disappointed with the outcome of the lessons: the pro because you are not willing or able to accomplish those high-level goals; you because these are not your personal goals.

The match between aspirations of teacher and pupil can be illustrated with a second scenario. You have decided to redo your game. You have organized your life so that you have the money, the time, and the energy to become a serious, low-handicap golfer. You talk to your pro about your goals. Remembering your high-handicap years, the pro views your aspirations as both unrealistic and unachievable. The pro may well be right, but right or not, goals are different for pupil and teacher.

In both of these illustrations, the question is not whether the pro is or is not a good teacher, nor whether you are or are not a good learner. Both you and the pro must agree upon compatible goals for you. You must have similar goals.

Do You Speak the Same Language?

A comfortable and effective working relationship between pupil and teacher is more than just a match in goals. Good instruction also involves how well pupil and teacher communicate and understand each other.

We have already described the effects of ambiguity and uncertainty on golfing performance. One thing to check out when choosing a pro is how well you understand what is being said. Does the pro use language and examples that you can understand? Is the pro able to provide different examples of the point to be learned, to show you different ways to master a certain technique?

Skilled and experienced people in any field develop a common language. It is sometimes called jargon, especially when it appears on government forms or in bureaucratic publications. While often annoying, from a psychological view, a common language or jargon helps people communicate more precisely with each other. However, communication depends upon everyone understanding the same language.

As we well know from government "technobabble," when language is not clear, it leads to misunderstanding, confusion, and frustration. Golf is no exception. The language of golf is specialized, different, and interesting. For experienced golfers and professionals, the terms have clear, unambiguous, and particular meanings. For many of us, the terms are confusing. Although we hear the words and we think we understand, we are often confused and are unable to synthesize the new ideas.

How's That Again?

One of the real problems in effective teaching in the classroom or on the golf course is to get a match in instructional language between pupil and teacher. This is not always easy to accomplish. To be comfortable with your pro, the language and the examples used in instruction have to make sense to you.

It's okay to keep questioning your pro, to ask for more examples, to insist that you understand before going to the next point. You may have to work with several pros before you find one who matches your particular instructional style.

Remember, the question is not whether the pro is a good teacher or a poor teacher, or whether you're a good learner or a poor learner. The question is whether this pro communicates effectively with you and whether you two are a good match.

Do You Follow the Same Drummer?

Like language, a match between pupil and pro in information-processing skills is essential for learning. When your information-processing system is overloaded, you function inefficiently and your performance deteriorates. This is dramatically illustrated in psychological laboratories and classrooms. It is also illustrated on the practice range. You need a teacher who can match your rate of information processing and who is sensitive to how much you can integrate in a given session.

The content and tempo of lessons depend on the abilities and skills of both the pupil and teacher. For a

golfer with a low handicap, a fast moving, highly organized, and content-loaded lesson may be extremely useful.
The low-handicap golfer has the skills, the technical
understanding, and the psychological stamina to profit
from large amounts of information at one time.

The same lesson may blow away the less skilled and less
experienced golfer. It may confuse rather than clarify. It
may overload the information-processing system of the
high handicapper to the point that her whole game gives
way. She may learn better from a slow-paced, low-key,
and low-demand lesson—the kind of lesson that may drive
a highly skilled golfer right up the wall.

The ability to recognize differences in information-
processing skills is an important part of teaching and learning. It helps the teacher decide how fast or how slow to
present new information. It determines in part how the
content of the lesson should be organized, how much content should be included, what order the material should be
presented, and how much the pupil can take in before
becoming overloaded and fatigued.

Professional golf teachers, like teachers in other fields,
differ in their abilities to recognize individual differences in
information-processing abilities of their pupils. It is
unrealistic to expect all professional golf teachers to be
equally adept at matching their instructional techniques to
each pupil's information-processing style and ability. It is
also unrealistic to expect that all pros will work equally effectively with all pupils.

The Decision is Yours

The important message is—find the right teacher for you.
The fact that you do not learn well from a particular
teacher, even though that pro has done wonders for your
friend's game, does not mean that you are a poor learner.
It merely means you and the pro didn't match—this was
the wrong teacher for you.

We have argued throughout this book that golfing performance and enjoyment are enhanced when you are in
charge of your game. Choosing the proper pro for you is
part of being in charge of your game.

Practice On And Off The Course

The old adage "practice makes perfect" has such a nice moral ring and is so ingrained in our thinking that most of us believe it. Given our limited golfing skills, it may also provide a single ray of hope that someday we, too, could be better golfers. Yet, we have all spent time on the practice range only to find our swings the same and our scores no lower. It is not surprising that most of us are not enthusiastic about practice.

Who, Me?

The unfortunate truth is that we don't know how to practice. Most women golfers approach practice from two extremes: too much or none at all. One golfer may go to the practice range or putting green and practice intensely but inefficiently. Another may procrastinate and never venture to the practice area. In either case, the golfer does not use the power of practice to the fullest.

In general, we expect too much from brief practice sessions, and we do not understand the long-range effects of practice. This is unfortunate because golfers can learn from psychological studies of practice. We know a good deal about how practice affects learning new information and how it helps in perfecting a physical or motor skill.

In a highly demanding activity such as golf, there isn't a simple, direct one-to-one relationship between amount of practice and amount of improvement. This is not to say that practice is not worthwhile or that you will play as well without practice as with regular practice. Sadly, however, each hour of practice does not translate to a one shot improvement in score. If it did, the practice ranges of the world would be filled day and night with improving golfers.

Practice is important, but its effects cannot be measured in direct increments of change. Be realistic. Four buckets of balls do not equal two shots off your score.

Practice Makes Perfect— But Not Quickly

Effects of practice may not be seen for considerable time—days or weeks after the actual practice took place. You may work very hard at getting your takeaway in good form and think you have it under control only to find that the new improved swing doesn't seem to make a difference on your tee shots when you play. You work hours on your putting stroke to find you still can't get the ball to the cup regularly.

Most of us expect immediate payoff after several hours of hard work. When that direct payoff isn't obvious immediately, we feel disappointed, frustrated, and unsure and inadequate. These feelings add to the load of tension we already carry around the golf course. As we have shown earlier, anxiety disrupts performance.

The fact that practice does not make perfect, or even lead to immediate dramatic improvement, does not mean you shouldn't practice. It does suggest that you need to know how to use practice to your advantage. What to practice and the timing of practice are two things that are especially important to consider.

The Bucket of Balls Syndrome

Why is it that most practice sessions are controlled by the size of the bucket of balls rather than by your own golfing needs? The idea seems to be to hit as many balls as far as you can, as fast as you can. This may be good for your figure or your respiration and may reduce your level of aggression, but it has little effect on the quality of your golf game. You need to be in charge of your practice sessions just as you are in charge of your play. Practice, like playing golf, requires thinking. You need to set realistic goals for practice and to allow time for the practice to be effective.

What should you practice? This is where the system of Personal Par is important. We showed you how to compute your Personal Par and how to use it to analyze your game—how to pinpoint your strengths and weaknesses so you'll know what to practice. There are different practice requirements depending on the task you want to learn. Decide what it is you want to learn or perfect so you'll know how to go about practicing it. You can learn a simple uncomplicated skill with a few heavy doses of work. A more complex skill which has many subcomponents requires more time and more practice sessions spaced over time. Remember, what is to be learned should determine how you practice.

Hang in There!

We don't need to remind you of the many demands of golf. It's not a simple game. No doubt that's what accounts for its charm and fascination as well as for its frustrations. Think of how complicated it is to hit a good shot. It requires coordination of eyes, body, and mind. It requires specific skills for holding a club, stance and balance, turning and pausing, swinging, and follow-through (as well as connecting with the ball). Some of these specific skills can be practiced and "overlearned" in a short time. We don't have to think them through every time. With concentrated practice, we can handle these automatic skills, and practice usually yields a direct payoff. You can improve specific skills with practice on the driving range.

The problem, however, is that golf is not just a matter of learning specific skills. Too often all the components of the act seem to work separately. You know all the specifics, but you can't get your act together. Coordination and integration of skills require a special practice plan.

Klutzes We Have Known

Remember when you learned to drive a car? You knew how to shift the years, how to work the clutch, how to steer, and how to use the accelerator. You know all the components of driving, yet you couldn't integrate the pieces because your feet weren't coordinated with your hands and eyes. The result was jerking, stalling, and considerable embarrassment.

Many of us also remember learning to ride a bicycle. We could pedal, steer, and maintain balance, but we couldn't put these segments together. The outcome was a precarious and short ride ending in total collapse and skinned elbows and knees.

The various components of driving and bicycling were learned relatively quickly and easily, but the integration of the components took a long time. However, once coordinated, the quality of performance improved dramatically. You weren't forced to pay attention to each specific.

Have You Considered Juggling?

In golf, integration of the various components and the smooth synthesis of specifics takes time, requiring continuing practice spaced out over weeks, months, even years. To try to practice everything in one big session is not effective use of practice time. More importantly, it may lead to fatigue and information overload, both factors which disrupt play.

Effective practice occurs when you know what it is you want to learn and when you have planned the right practice schedule. You may be able to work out the bugs in your grip or putting stance in a single practice session, but don't be disappointed that the session doesn't improve your overall game or lower your score.

Integration of skills requires practice spaced over time. In this sense, you are engaged in spaced practice every time you play. Every round is an opportunity to analyze your game and to practice certain skills. Psychologically, time on the course and time on the practice range are both useful ways to understand and to improve your game. Remember, when planning your practice, think of two things: What are you trying to learn? What is the best schedule to learn it?

Try a Little Mental Practice

True, we could be better golfers if we practiced more. Realistically, time on the practice range is limited for most women. A good deal of our involvement with golf, when we think about, analyze, or even fantasize about our games, comes off the course.

Fortunately, we know from psychological research that not all improvement must occur with club in hand. A number of things can be accomplished away from the course which will actually help you play better when you are there.

We are not referring to general programs of health and exercise, although you are obviously more apt to play well if you feel fit and have plenty of energy. Nor are we talking about specific golf exercises such as hand strengthening or finger exercises, although these, too, may lead to better technique and play. What we are talking about is mental practice.

In Your Mind's Eye

The coordination of skills so important in golf go on even when you are not playing. Indeed, psychologists have shown that performance sometimes improves when there is a break in an activity. Psychologists call this *reminiscence*. It means that performance may be better after some time away from an activity than it was immediately after learning or after practice occurred. A vacation away from the activity may actually improve your performance.

Applied to golf, reminiscence suggests that there is continuing learning and integration going on, even if you are not actually out on the golf course or on the practice range. Time away from golf is not just an interruption or deterrent to your game. It provides opportunity for the various segments of your game to come together and to meld. Golf is a complex game which requires coordination and integration of intellect and physical skills. Studies of reminiscence suggest that we need time for the different components to settle in and to become coordinated.

1ST TEE
300 YARDS
PAR 4

Time Away Spells Relief

Time away also provides you a chance to mentally review and analyze your game, to identify consistent mistakes in judgment or in execution, and to assess and evaluate your assumptions and expectancies.

Time away is an opportunity for mental practice. Mental practice is thinking about your game. Let's consider some of the ways mental practice or thinking about our game may help.

What Is Mental Practice?

Mental practice involves replaying a round in your head, visualizing the flight of a particularly good shot, and remembering the feeling of a well-hit ball. Mental practice also involves review and analysis of your playing strategies, as well as your club and shot selection. Mental practice helps you identify your strengths and weaknesses as a golfer and allows you to determine the appropriateness of your golfing goals.

In an earlier chapter, we stressed that golf is a whole brain activity which requires information processing in both cerebral hemispheres. Mental practice uses both analytic and integrative strategies. The analytic approach helps you identify the problem spots; the integrative approach helps you put your game back together.

Let's look at how the system of Personal Par helps mental practice. When you update your Personal Pars for each hole, you can see where you're having problems and where your playing has improved. Given the many demands of golf, it is clear that we can all profit from mental practice. Time on the course is not the only way to better play.

A War Story

Here are familiar examples that illustrate how mental review and practice help. After a mental replay of several rounds, Barbara realized that she consistently played the 9th hole badly. Nine is not a physically demanding hole, and Barbara thought she could play it well. Yet, she consistently three-putted. As on many courses, golfers usually detour for coffee and snacks between nines. For Barbara this anticipated break interrupted her concentration and led to poor performance. Recognizing that her attention was easily disrupted on this hole, Barbara increased her effort to keep her mind on golf, skipped the confusion of the snack bar, and improved her ability to maintain her concentration. Having identified the problem through mental replay, she was able to work out some ways to cope with the potential disruption: She visualized the hole and the way she wanted to play it; she really concentrated on her preshot routine; and she actively avoided distracting conversation.

More War Stories

When Carol checked her recent scores against her Personal Pars, she found she was consistently ever her par on the short holes. This was puzzling as she was hitting the ball well and should have been playing to her Personal Par of 5. Mentally replaying the holes, she realized that she was close to the hole in 2 as expected, but that she consistently loused up her third shot. She had been trying to follow the advice of a television commentator who suggested a sand wedge for this shot. For Carol the instructions were ambiguous, and although she concentrated, most of the time she couldn't execute the shot. After her mental review, Carol switched to a club she knew how to use. Her scores on the short holes began to match her Personal Pars.

Self-Analysis and Self-Realization

Mental review is a kind of practice. It helps you identify poor decisions and bad playing strategies. Think back over your last several rounds. Do you find that in certain situations or holes you consistently underclub? Do you frequently have to take an extra shot near the green because you were short with an iron that "should" have reached the pin? Are you reasonably consistent off the tee but find that your fairway woods are almost always misplayed? Is it the pitch-and-run shot to the green that you flub? Are you inconsistent with 3- to 4-foot putts? Recognition of your problems gives you direction for what should be practiced, and also alerts you to the need for particular attention on these shots.

We have already noted that most of us cannot sustain attention for 4 or more consecutive hours. The middle of a round is no place to review and reflect on previous rounds or shots; you need all your attention and effort for the shot you are preparing to hit. Mental review of the round after you have played it allows you to rethink each shot, to identify errors in judgment, and to visualize the shot with the correct club. There is considerable learning going on as you reconstruct the shot mentally, and this insight and mental practice will pay off when you are faced with the actual situation in another round. The mental practice makes the hole more familiar and more easily played. Mental practice prepares you for the demands of particular holes and shots.

Personal Par Helps

Mental practice helps you set realistic and positive goals. In our system of Personal Par, we have stressed that optimal goals, neither too low nor too high, lead to improved play. A tough problem with setting optimal goals is facing up to our limitations as golfers. Most of us delude ourselves to think that we are far better golfers than we are. Mental practice helps you set optimal levels of Personal Par—levels that are both realistic and challenging.

One Last Shot

We began this book with the belief that women golfers, whatever the level of their skill, want to play better golf. Most of us take our games seriously. Serious doesn't necessarily mean that you have a low handicap or are heading for the tour. Serious does mean wanting to play better; it means caring about golf and your play. In that sense, we are all serious golfers whether our actual scores average 80, 100, or 120.

Fortunately for most of us, psychology can help serious golfers. From a psychological perspective, we know that women play better golf and have more fun when they feel in charge of their games. Being in charge means choosing where and when you play, playing with people who enjoy the game the way you do, setting your own goals, and playing your own game. Being in charge means using psychology to your advantage.

Personal Par is a system based on the psychology of golf: It will help you use your skills by controlling your golfing motivations and anxieties; it will help you set positive and enhancing goals; and it will help you understand your own expectations and aspirations. Most of all, it will lead to better play and to more enjoyment.

Remember, motivation is not just trying hard. Expectations, attributions, and locus of control are all important for golfers. Your expectations for your play, your attribu-

tions about your successes and failures, and your feelings of being in charge of your play all affect your self-confidence and your views of yourself as a golfer. But your expectations and goals may not match your skills, and this leads to anxiety and tensions which affect play.

Too much tension leads to disruption and poor play; too little tension leads to lack of involvement, to boredom, and to poor play. Tension also disrupts your ability to sustain attention over a round. The best golf is played under conditions of optimal tension, at the middle of the inverted U, where anxieties result in heightened attention, increased arousal, and better concentration.

Whether you are an Olympic athlete, a touring golf pro, or a 35 handicapper, you are affected by psychological pressures. The trick is to control and to direct these pressures and tensions. Disruptive tension can be controlled through recognition of the sources of anxiety: unreachable goals, information overload, ambiguity of information, and oversensitivity to distractions. Playing to a system of Personal Par will help you manage yourself and your game.

Here are some suggestions to get you started in the Personal Par system. Some of these things are done away from the course before you actually start to play. Others are helpful during the time you are playing. Still others are hints about how to think through your game after you have finished a round. These are simple suggestions which

will improve your understanding of your game and of
yourself as a golfer.

Par-Snippets

Before You Play

Establish honest Personal Pars for each hole on your home
course. Make your Personal Pars real based on your four
most recent rounds—no shoulds, oughts, mights, or even
"occasionallies."

Get organized to give yourself a break: Set a tee time
that is reasonable; sign up with playing partners you enjoy; get to the course so you have a little alone time on the
putting green; go through your warmup routine;
disengage from your other world.

While You Play

Remember your game plan; you are playing to your Personal Pars not someone else's. Play each hole as if it is the
only hole on the course. Don't add up your total score until you finish the round.

Manage your attention; ease off after each shot and
smell the flowers. Crank up your attention as you approach the next shot; note where you are what shot will be
reasonable for you. Be realistic; don't overanalyze.

Enjoy success; rejoice at Personal Pars and personal
birdies.

After You Play

Rethink your round. Remember what you did well; identify what went wrong; think about consistencies in good
and bad shots; review what you need to practice.

Update your Personal Par records and make adjustments
where your pars have changed.

Get on the phone; make your next starting time.

It's a Fun Game

Golf is fun and we should enjoy every round fully. Each
round is different, filled with triumphs and tragedies. Each

shot is a challenge. Being tested is part of what makes golf fun and what brings us back time after time. If every shot were easy, the game would be boring and uninteresting. If every shot were impossible, the game would be defeating. That's where the notion of Personal Par becomes important. It is a system which allows you to manage your game.

Remember

You have greater control over your game when you understand your motivations for playing.

Your peak performance is at the middle of the anxiety curve.

You play best when you set realistic goals.

The system of Personal Par provides a psychological perspective that adds up to one major rule—YOU ARE IN CHARGE OF YOUR GAME.

Have Fun

HOLE	1	2	3	4	5	6	7	8	9	10	11	12	13	14	15	16	17	18
DATE																		
TOTAL																		
AVERAGE																		
PUTTS	+2	+2	+2	+2	+2	+2	+2	+2	+2	+2	+2	+2	+2	+2	+2	+2	+2	+2
PERSONAL PAR																		

HOLE	1	2	3	4	5	6	7	8	9	10	11	12	13	14	15	16	17	18
DATE																		
TOTAL																		
AVERAGE																		
PUTTS	+2	+2	+2	+2	+2	+2	+2	+2	+2	+2	+2	+2	+2	+2	+2	+2	+2	+2
PERSONAL PAR																		